THE FIRST ROCK STAR ON MARS

D1097247

by James DiNanno

Dedicated to Caden James DiNanno

The teacher said, "when you grow up what do you want to be? Answer the question realistically."

"A salesman, a dentist, maybe a plumber?
An accountant if you're good with numbers."

I thought about every possibility.
These are fine jobs, but they're not for me.

I looked and looked at the list.

But what I want to be is a thing she missed ...

When I grow up, I'll be the first singer to play on Mars.
They'll arrive at my concert in flying cars.

They'll sing from their seats on top of stars
to the first rock star to perform on Mars.

The teacher said "Pick another one.
The thing you talk about just can't be done!"

Didn't Neil Armstrong walk on the moon?
Before he did, I bet they called him a buffoon.

When the Wright brothers said they would learn to fly
I bet everyone said, "Stop telling lies!"

So go ahead and tell me the answer is no.
So one day I can say I told you so !

Let's skip to the future, 2045.

Beyond the satellites way up in the sky.

The venue is a big red place
somewhere in the endless space.

I sing on Mars. Yes, it's true.
Everyone sings along, my teacher too.

I am the first singer to play on Mars.
They arrive at my concert in flying cars..

They sing from their seats, on top of stars
to the first rock star to perform on Mars.

James DiNanno

James DiNanno is the owner of PlaybookU and Little PlaybookU. The companies empower children and adults to master their life goals. James spent his teens and early 20's as the touring drummer in rock bands Silhouette Rising, The Life Electric and Callisto. In the last decade, he and his wife founded and took ownership of multiple businesses; Meritage Entertainment, Ambient Force and Boston GIF.

James currently lives in Exeter, NH with his wife, son and 2 standard poodles.

When James was in elementary school, a teacher told him in front of the class that a career as a professional rock drummer and DJ was not realistic. Because of his parents' encouragement, he went on to successfully pursue both of those dreams.

This book is dedicated to James' son Caden and all children with big dreams. It was written as a reminder that the first step to achieving is believing. "Don't let anyone tell you that you cannot do something. I believe that you can."

Luciana Guerra

Luciana was born in Argentina. She's been drawing for her entire life and went to The Fine Arts University. She attended both Julián Usandizaga's and Rodolfo Perassi's workshop.
Her practice continued over the next decade while living in Buenos Aires.
Luciana studied Museology, Museum Guide and drawing and painting with Jorge Mansueto until 2016. Last year she attended Eduardo Stupía's workshop at Di Tella University.
Currently residing in Rosario, her painting and drawing continues in Paula Grazzini's workshop.
Between 2002 and 2008, she taught drawing, painting and sculpture workshops locally.
Last year she was one of the illustrators to win the Local Story Contest by the EMR (Rosario Public Publishing).

Through her career, Luciana has won several awards such as the First Prize for Painting at the National Salon of Tornquist Bank in Buenos Aires, First Prize for Painting in the National Salon of the APS Foundation in Buenos Aires and the First Prize for Painting from the Goethe Foundation in Rosario, among others. She participates in individual and collective art exhibitions from 2006 to the present day.

Made in the USA
Monee, IL
13 December 2020